James Stewart

By Jeff Savage

Lerner Publications Company • Minneapolis

To Redding's fearless Sam Schmidt. Soar high!

Text copyright © 2008 by Jeff Savage

Lerner Publications Company
A division of Lerner Publishing Group, Inc.
241 First Avenue North
Minneapolis, MN 55401 U.S.A.

Website address: www.lernerbooks.com

Library of Congress Cataloging-in-Publication Data

Savage, Jeff, 1961–
    James Stewart / by Jeff Savage.
       p.   cm. — (Amazing athletes)
    Includes index.
    ISBN 978–0–8225–7663–1 (lib. bdg. : alk. paper)
    1. Stewart, James, 1985–—Juvenile literature. 2. Motorcyclists—United States—Biography—Juvenile literature. 3. Motocross—Juvenile literature. I. Title.
GV1060.2.S84S39 2008
796.7'5092—dc22 [B]   2007000760

Manufactured in the United States of America
1 2 3 4 5 6 – DP – 13 12 11 10 09 08

TABLE OF CONTENTS

James Stewart (number 259) takes the lead. Ricky Carmichael (4) and Chad Reed (22) follow close behind.

A SUPER RACE

James Stewart roared out of the gate on his lime green motorcycle. He swept around the first turn. He was in front of the other racers. Suddenly, James noticed something was wrong. "I didn't have a front brake," he said.

How could James race 20 laps with a broken brake system? He would surely crash. But James never gives up. He held onto the lead as he went around the sharp turns. He added to his lead as he sailed over the **whoop-de-doos**. He twisted the **throttle** and powered his Kawasaki KX250 down the **straightaway** at 70 miles per hour.

Not even a broken brake system can keep James from charging all the way to the end.

James holds off Carmichael and Reed through another tight turn.

James was racing in the 2005 **American Motorcyclist Association (AMA) 250cc Supercross** series. More than 43,276 fans had packed Texas Stadium in Irving, Texas, to see the greatest Supercross riders in the world. **Veteran** racers like Ricky Carmichael, Jeremy McGrath, and Chad Reed were expected to fight for the win. But James Stewart had other ideas.

James's nickname is Bubba. The other riders knew Bubba was fearless. But he was still just a teenager and a **rookie**. This was only his third race in the top 250cc series. How could he win?

James skidded around a **hairpin** turn. His rear tire sprayed dirt behind him. James was confident, even without his front brake. He used

racing tricks like the "Bubba Scrub." He flew lower off jumps than other riders did. He tilted his bike sideways in the air. The trick made him go faster.

James flies over a jump at top speed.

James held the lead. He crossed the finish line first! He became the first African American in the 32-year history of Supercross to win a top series race. "I'm so happy!" said James afterward. "I have my first win, and now I know how it feels."

James raises a fist in the air to celebrate his first 250cc Supercross victory!

James's dad, James Stewart Sr., enjoyed motocross racing as a kid.

BORN WITH A BIKE

James Stewart Jr. was born December 21, 1985, in Bartow, Florida. Even before he was born, James was full of energy. His father, James Sr., said: "I'd press on my wife Sonya's stomach, and he would move around like he was dancing." His nickname at birth was Boogie.

James's father was a former **motocross (MX)** rider. He raced at local tracks. When James was just two days old, his father took him for his first motorcycle ride. On his third birthday, James got his first motorcycle—a Yamaha PW50. His father taught him how to ride safely. By age four, James began racing. "I wasn't good when I first started," he said. "But I always wanted to be better than everybody."

James was seven when his little brother, Malcolm, was born. Malcolm later would race motorcycles too. By this time, James was already proving to be a special rider. He was filling his bedroom with trophies. He knew his future was motocross.

As a kid, James was a fan of veteran racer Jeff "Chicken" Matiasevich. James started calling himself Baby Chicken.

When James was seven years old, Kawasaki signed him to a long-term **contract**. Kawasaki would give James bikes and equipment. They would pay him to race for them. For James, it was a dream come true.

The Stewart family bought a motor home. They traveled along the East Coast for racing events. James did his homework in the motor home. Kids at school were jealous that James got to travel and miss school. They picked on him. The teasing hurt James. He tried to prove himself. In school, he raced classmates during tests to finish first. "I slammed the pencil down so that everybody knew I was done," he said. "I would yell 'Done!'"

James was tearing up motocross racetracks before he reached his teen years.

RISING STAR

James lived for motocross. He hurried home from school each day to ride. His father had built two racetracks. One was a motocross track with hills and long straightaways. He also built a shorter Supercross track with steep jumps and sharp turns. The practice paid off. By age 12, James was winning nearly every AMA event he entered.

James had worked his way up from 50cc motorcycles to the faster 125cc bikes. By this time, his friends were calling him Bubba. No one knew why. James said: "A typical Bubba looks like an older white gentleman, kind of fat, who lives on a farm, has a toothpick and wears overalls and a straw hat."

In the years 2000 and 2001, James entered 76 races. He won 72 of them. He set the AMA record for most **amateur** national championships with 11. He broke the record of 9 held by Ricky Carmichael.

At age 16, James turned **pro**. Companies paid him money to sponsor their products. His image was put on Xbox and PlayStation2 video games. He earned enough money to buy a big house for his family in Haines City, Florida. The new place had a 65-acre backyard.

Fans watch in wonder as James flies high over a jump at a motocross event in 2002.

James roars through the mud on his way to another motocross win.

James was homeschooled so that he could ride during the day. He rode for hours on his three dirt practice tracks. James even practiced celebrating while flying through the air by whipping his rear wheel out and pointing at an imaginary crowd.

James won his second pro race, in San Diego. The win made him the youngest rider ever to win an AMA 125cc Supercross main event. He was just 16 years and 22 days old. James finished the season in second place in the **points standings**.

James has been a big winner in both motocross and Supercross.

The 2002 AMA 125cc national motocross series came next. James roared past the other riders to win 10 of the 12 events. His 10 victories were a record. He was the youngest ever to win a series title. "I'm a little surprised at the success," James admitted. "But it was always my goal to be that fast. I knew I could be."

James soars through a practice session at the 2003 AMA National Motocross Championships.

MAKING THE JUMP

In 2003, *Teen People* magazine named James one of "20 Teens Who Will Change the World." A newspaper headline called him "The Tiger Woods of Supercross."

James *(right)* celebrates another win with his good friend Cincinnati Reds outfielder Ken Griffey Jr.

James became friends with Woods and other sports superstars like baseball's Ken Griffey Jr. and basketball's Michael Jordan. Griffey liked to ride motorcycles with James in his backyard and play video games with him. He called James "the **Jackie Robinson** of his sport."

James's parents kept their son grounded. "We don't listen to the hype," said James's father. "We tell James, 'Do what you know best, and your best is on the bike.'"

James showed what he could do again in 2003. He won seven straight Supercross races. But in an event in Las Vegas, he crashed and broke his collarbone. He had surgery and then left the hospital in a hurry to attend an awards ceremony. "I had a beautiful date," James said. "I had to go." He missed six weeks of racing. When he returned to action, he won the next 12 races.

Fans are getting used to seeing James's smiling face on the winner's podium at Supercross races.

James raises his arms in the air after another amazing performance.

Most people thought James was ready to move up to the top class—the 250cc series. James decided to wait. "I want to get more experience and try to win more races so that I'm ready when I step up," he said. "I want people to be shaking in their boots."

In Supercross, James races against the top riders in the world. But James usually comes out on top.

In 2004, James won 11 of 12 motocross events. In the last two years, he had racked up 47 wins—another AMA record. He won every race he finished. He lost only when he crashed. He was ready for 250cc bikes. Top riders knew what they were in for. "The kid is awesome," said seven-time champion Jeremy McGrath. "He's got killer style and real good technique. And he's a nice kid."

Tickets were sold out one month in advance of the first event of the 2005 AMA Supercross season. More than 45,000 people stood in a heavy rain in Anaheim, California, to see a royal battle.

Ricky Carmichael had won every Supercross race the year before. "He's the rookie and I'm the veteran," said Carmichael. "So it should be interesting to see how well he will do." The race was a crazy mess. The dirt track looked like a mud bog. The racers tried to keep their bikes upright as they slogged through the mud. James finished in fifth place, two spots behind Carmichael.

The second event of the season was held in Phoenix, Arizona. Disaster struck during the final practice session before the race. James crashed and broke his left arm. He was taken to the hospital for surgery. He had to miss the next nine events.

James rejoined the series in Orlando, Florida. He finished third. The following week in Texas he won! He won twice more in 2005 to prove he could compete with the greatest. "People expect me to win now," James said. "There are greater expectations, and my job is to make sure people believe."

James *(left)* talks with legendary rider Ricky Carmichael after a race.

James wore the number 3 on his bike when he competed in the international Motocross des Nations event in 2006.

FINISHING STRONG

James is just five feet seven inches tall. He weighs 155 pounds. But his body is packed with muscles. He is strong enough to handle even the heavy 450cc motorcycles that the Supercross series rolled out for 2006.

He proved it by winning the 2006 World Supercross GP Championship in Las Vegas. He shot out to the lead and held on to beat Ricky Carmichael and the rest of the field. James and the great Carmichael stood together at the finish line and bowed to the crowd. Then they hugged. "You are the most fun person I have ever raced with in my life," James said. Carmichael said the same words back to James.

James poses with his miniature bulldog.

In 2007, James was the fastest man on the track in nearly every race. Only Carmichael and Chad Reed came close to keeping up.

James had one of his greatest rides in Orlando, Florida. Carmichael was retiring, and wanted to go out on top. But James chased his hero through the whole race. He passed him on the final laps to steal another win! James finished the season with his first AMA Supercross title.

James is rich and famous. He earns more than $4 million a year from **sponsorships**. He owns 17 cars, including a yellow Lamborghini, a Porsche 911, and three Chevrolet Camaro

Z28s. He keeps them in his garage in Haines City. He carries his pet miniature bulldog with him in a $1,340 Louis Vuitton bag. Pictures of James appear on the cover of magazines. "I don't get too hyped about all that stuff," he says. "I take this as my job, and it's cool."

James celebrates his first win at the Daytona Supercross in the 450cc class in 2007.

James focuses on riding. He trains hard at his home in Haines City. The whole Stewart family helps out. His dad works to maintain the dirt tracks. His mom washes his motorcycles. His little brother, Malcolm, rides too.

"I'm glad I'm the first African American and the youngest rider to win a Supercross race," James says. "But we all look the same under the helmet. To me, it's more important that I do it for myself. I want to be the best, and I won't settle for anything less."

James shows off during a practice session in his backyard in Haines City, Florida.

Selected Career Highlights

2007 Won AMA Supercross championship
Won FIM World Supercross GP championship

2006 Won World Supercross GP
Championship
Led United States to victory in
Motocross des Nations

2005 Won three events in 250cc
AMA Supercross series

2004 Won record 47 125cc
Supercross and MX events
over two years
Won record 11 (out of 12)
125cc AMA MX events

2003 Won AMA 125cc West Region
Supercross series title
Won AMA 125cc East Region Supercross series title
Won AMA 125cc motocross series title

2002 Became the youngest AMA 125cc motocross series national
champion ever
Won record 10 (out of 12) 125cc AMA MX events
Became first African American AMA champion
Named 2002 AMA Motocross/Supercross Rookie of the Year

2001 Finished amateur riding career with record 11 national titles

Glossary

amateur: someone who receives no money for competing in a sporting event

American Motorcyclist Association (AMA): a group that organizes many professional and amateur motorcycle events in the United States

contract: a written agreement

hairpin: an extremely sharp turn that can resemble the shape of a hairpin

motocross (MX): a motorcycle race held outdoors on a long dirt track marked with big hills and wide turns

points standings: ranking of riders based on points earned. In racing, riders collect points based on their place of finish. A rider's points for each event are added to their total to determine the overall series winner.

pro: a rider who is allowed to receive prize money for competing

Jackie Robinson: the first African American to play Major League Baseball

rookie: a first-year rider

sponsorships: deals in which a company gives a rider money or equipment

straightaway: a long, straight part of a racetrack

Supercross: a motorcycle race held in a stadium or arena on a dirt track featuring steep jumps and sharp turns

throttle: the device on the end of the right handlebar that the rider rotates to provide power

250cc: 250 cubic centimeters. The size of a motorcycle's engine is often measured in cubic centimeters. In Supercross, the competition is usually divided between bikes with 125cc, 250cc, and 450cc engines.

veteran: an experienced rider

whoop-de-dos: a series of humps on a Supercross track

Further Reading & Websites

Raby, Philip, and Simon Nix. *Motorbikes*. Minneapolis: LernerSports, 1999.

Savage, Jeff. *Travis Pastrana*. Minneapolis: Lerner Publications Company, 2006.

American Motorcyclist Association
http://www.ama-cycle.org
The AMA's website provides motorcycle fans with schedules and results of all races, as well as features and information on riders.

James Stewart Online
http://www.jamesstewartonline.com
This is James's official website, featuring a biography, photos, records, and information about James.

Sports Illustrated for Kids
http://www.sikids.com
The Sports Illustrated for Kids website covers all sports, including Supercross and motocross racing.

Index

Photo Acknowledgments

Photographs are used with the permission of: © Steve Bruhn, pp. 4, 5, 6, 7, 8, 9, 19, 21, 23, 25, 27; © Ryan Mahoney-Photocross.net, pp. 12, 15, 16, 24, 29; © Jeff Kardas/Getty Images, pp. 14, 17; © Steve Bruhn/Getty Images, pp. 18, 20; AP Photo/Brian Myrick, p. 28.

Front cover: AP Photo/Brian Myrick

TOP 50 QUESTIONS

Poisonous Animals

SEYMOUR SIMON

SCHOLASTIC INC.

New York   Toronto   London   Auckland   Sydney
Mexico City   New Delhi   Hong Kong   Buenos Aires

To Grandkids and grand kids everywhere

Acknowledgments

Special thanks to Jenne Abramowitz for her terrific editing, to Janet Kusmierski for her excellent design, and to Alison Kolani for her skillful copyediting. The author is grateful to David Reuther for his editorial and design suggestions, as well as his enthusiasm for this project. Also, many thanks to Gina Shaw and Suzanne Nelson at Scholastic Inc., for their generous help.

Photo Credits

Front cover: © David A. Northcott/CORBIS; back cover and page 16: © William Dow/CORBIS; page 1: © Aaron Horowitz/CORBIS; page 3: © Peter B. Kaplan/Photo Researcher, Inc.; page 4: © Martin Harvey/CORBIS; page 5 (top): © Chas. & Elizabeth Schwartz Trust/AnimalsAnimals; page 5 (bottom): © Royalty Free/CORBIS; pages 6 and 24 (bottom): © Zig Leszczynski/AnimalsAnimals; page 7: © Color-Pic/ AnimalsAnimals; pages 7 (spot) and 13 (bottom): © Joe McDonald/CORBIS; page 8 (top): © OSF/Michael Fogden/AnimalsAnimals; page 8 (bottom): © Michael & Patricia Fogden/CORBIS; pages 9, 30 (bottom) and 31: © Tom McHugh/Photo Researchers, Inc.; pages 10: © Anthony Bannister/ABPL/ Photo Researchers, Inc.; page 11 (top): © Michael Fogden/ AnimalsAnimals; page 11 (bottom): © Austin J. Stevens/AnimalsAnimals; page 12: © Gary Bell/Taxi/Getty Images; page 13 (bottom): © Anthony Bannister/Photo Researchers, Inc.; page 14 (top): © Gerry Ellis/Getty Images; page 14 (bottom): © James H. Robinson/Photo Researchers, Inc.; page 15 (top): © G.W. Willis/AnimalsAnimals; page 15 (bottom): © A.N.T./Photo Researchers, Inc.; page 17 (top): © Scott Camazine/Photo Researchers, Inc.; page 17 (spot): © Eric V. Grave/Photo Researchers, Inc.; page 17 (bottom): © Dr. John Brackenbury/ Photo Researchers, Inc.; page 18 (top): © Stephen Dalton/AnimalsAnimals; page 18 (bottom): © Roget DeLaHarpe/ABPL/AnimalsAnimals; page 19: © James Robinson/AnimalsAnimals; page 20: © Dr. Paul Zahi/Photo Researchers, Inc.; page 21 (top): © Richard Cummins/CORBIS; page 21 (bottom): © Mark Moffett/ScienceFaction; page 22: © Tim Flach/Stone/Getty Images; page 23: © Doug Wechsler/AnimalsAnimals; page 24 (top): © Bob Elsdale/Image Bank/Getty Images; page 25 (top): © Mary Beth Angelo/Photo Researchers, Inc.; page 25 (bottom): © James Watt/AnimalsAnimals; page 26 (top): © Jeffrey L. Rotman/CORBIS; page 26 (bottom): © Jeff Rotman/Getty Images; page 27: © Stuart Westmoreland/ScienceFaction; page 28: © Peter Skinner/Photo Researchers, Inc.; page 29: © Gary Bell/zefa/CORBIS; page 30 (top): © Jeff Rotman/Photo Researchers, Inc.

Images of the animals in this book do not appear at actual size.

ISBN-13: 978-0-439-79600-2
ISBN-10: 0-439-79600-8

15 14 13   40   11 12/0

Printed in the U.S.A.
First printing, March 2007

1 What kinds of animals are poisonous?

From killer bees and black widow spiders to cobras and lionfish, thousands of different animals are poisonous or venomous.

② Is there a difference between poison and venom?

Sometimes people use *venom* to talk about a poison produced inside the body of an animal. This animal purposefully bites or injects venom into the body of another animal. *Poison* sometimes means "something that is harmful to eat or take in." So, for example, a venomous snake might bite you, but you might accidentally eat a poisonous mushroom.

③ Can you tell if a snake is venomous?

Venomous snakes look very different from each other. Rattlesnakes have triangular-shaped heads and cobras have wide hoods. But equally venomous coral snakes, taipans, and mambas have heads that look similar to many non-venomous snakes. So it's best not to handle any snake you find in nature.

4 How do a snake's fangs work?

Venomous snakes use fangs to inject their poison. Fangs are a special pair of hollow or grooved teeth with tubes inside. They connect to sacs of venom in the snake's cheeks.

5 What is the world's most venomous snake?

The 12 foot long taipan of Australia and New Guinea has the most feared bite of any venomous snake. It can strike a half-dozen times before the victim has a chance to move. A taipan's half-inch long fangs inject enough venom in a single bite to kill 30 people.

Which American snakes are venomous?

America is home to about two dozen different kinds of rattlesnakes. The copperhead, the water moccasin or cottonmouth, the coral snake, and the yellow-bellied sea snake can also be found in America.

Copperhead

⑦ Where do rattlesnakes live?

Rattlesnakes live in many different places. They are found in Canada, Mexico, and all across the United States. Many live in the deserts of the American Southwest, but some also live in grasslands, forests, and mountains. Rattlesnakes prey upon rabbits, prairie dogs, ground squirrels, small lizards, and birds. The eastern diamondback rattler is the largest venomous snake in North America. It's over eight feet long with fangs up to one inch.

⑧ How does a rattlesnake rattle?

A rattlesnake's rattle is made of special interlocking scales at the end of its tail. A rattlesnake can shake its tail as fast as 60 times a second. When it does, the scales hit each other and make a noise. The noise may not sound like a rattle at all. Some people think it sounds more like a buzzing insect. It's loud enough to hear from 100 feet away.

Zoom Fact: Rattlesnakes are deaf and cannot hear their own or another snake's rattle.

⑨ What's a sidewinder?

A sidewinder is a rattlesnake that lives in the deserts of the Southwest. Its name comes from the way it moves across the sand. Only two points of the snake's body touch the ground, one near the front, the other near the rear. The snake moves sideways leaving J-shaped tracks in the sand.

⑩ How deadly are coral snakes?

Coral snakes are highly venomous. They are a kind of elapid, which is a family of snakes that includes cobras, sea snakes, and mambas. Coral snakes rarely bite humans, but when they do they can cause death

unless the victim is treated with antivenom. The common coral snake is usually less than three feet long, and has bands of red, yellow, and black covering its body.

11 What is antivenom?

Antivenom is a fluid that is injected into people to protect them against the effects of a snake's venom. Antivenom is made from the venom of a snake in a process called *milking*. The venom is diluted to make it weaker, and then injected into a horse or a goat. The animal builds up resistance to the venom. Its blood becomes rich in antibodies, which fight the harmful effects of venom. These antibodies are used to make the antivenom.

12 What are some different kinds of cobras?

The king cobra is the largest and heaviest poisonous animal in the world. Adults often reach a length of 14 feet. They can inject more venom than any other snake, over two teaspoonfuls, enough to kill a human being or other large animal. King cobras, spitting cobras, and Indian cobras live in Southeast Asia, India, China, and some nearby islands. Two African cobras are also called spitting cobras.

13 Are baby cobras deadly?

Baby cobras, called hatchlings, have full-strength venom. They can inject enough venom to kill a human.

14 How deadly is the black mamba?

The black mamba is the largest and most feared poisonous snake in Africa. It is a slender, fast-moving snake that can grow up to 14 feet long. The mamba has large fangs that are located far forward in its mouth. It often stays hidden from view among rocks or long grasses, so it's easy to stumble upon a mamba accidentally. Then the mamba strikes quickly and injects a deadly nerve venom that can kill a person in minutes.

15 What is the death adder?

The Australian death adder is not really an adder at all. It's a member of the elapid family, along with cobras and mambas. It is a short, thick snake about three feet long. It usually stays still, waiting for prey to come near. Its bite is very dangerous and can cause death in humans.

16 Which venomous snake has the longest fangs?

The Gaboon viper has the longest fangs of any snake in the world. This six foot long snake has two inch long fangs. The snake folds its fangs into the back of its mouth when they are not in use, and then snaps them out in an instant to strike.

17 Are there any venomous sea snakes?

All of the 50 different kinds of sea snakes are venomous. Their fangs and venom are much like cobras and other elapids. The fangs are hollow, always upright, and located in the front of their mouths. One kind of sea snake has venom that is 50 times more powerful than that of the king cobra. Few people are bitten by sea snakes, but they do pose some danger when they get entangled in fishing nets.

18 Are all spiders poisonous?

Almost all of the 50,000 different kinds of spiders are poisonous. But in most cases, the poison is not dangerous to people. Most spiders' fangs are too small to break through human skin. Even if they do bite

a person, most spiders don't produce enough venom to cause more than a small irritation of the skin.

19 How do spiders inject their venom?

Spiders inject venom through curved fangs and poison glands in their jaws. By squeezing these muscles around the glands, a spider can regulate the amount of venom it injects. The venom paralyzes or kills their prey, usually insects or other small animals.

13

20 Are tarantulas deadly?

Tarantulas are usually hairy, have two big fangs, and can be as large as a dinner plate. They hunt by stalking and slowly creeping up on insects, small birds, and mammals. Tarantulas look frightening but they rarely bite people. And even if they do bite, their poison usually has little effect on a person.

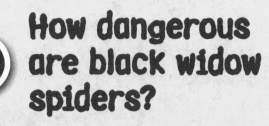

21 How dangerous are black widow spiders?

Black widows are found all over the world, including the United States. When threatened, a black widow will seldom bite. Bites occur when someone steps on a black widow accidentally. The female black widow is much larger than the male and her bite is much deadlier. Most people recover from a black widow bite, and only a few people die from them each year.

Is there another dangerous American spider?

22

The brown recluse, or fiddleback spider, is found throughout the United States, Mexico, and Central America. It is as poisonous as the black widow, but less likely to encounter people because it hunts at night. The bite of a brown recluse can result in a painful wound. But death is rare. Still, a brown recluse bite may take as long as six to eight weeks to heal.

Which is the deadliest spider in the world?

23

The deadliest spider in the world is the funnel-web spider of Australia. It is about the size of a large grape and has fangs 1/3 of an inch long. The venom is dangerous enough to kill an untreated child in an hour and an adult in a few days.

24 How dangerous are scorpions?

Scorpions are venomous arachnids that are found throughout the deserts of the southwestern United States, Mexico, and parts of Africa and the Middle East. In Mexico alone, more than 70,000 people are stung by scorpions each year, resulting in more than 1,000 deaths. Scorpions inject their venom through stingers at the tips of their tails. Even baby scorpions are venomous at birth.

25 Which are the deadliest scorpions?

The deadliest scorpion in the United States is the small bark scorpion that lives in Arizona. But, the four inch long Sahara scorpion that lives in the deserts of Northern Africa has the deadliest sting of any scorpion in the world. One out of every five stings results in death.

INSECTS

26 How do insects inject venom?

Insects such as bees, wasps, and hornets use stingers to inject their venom. Bees have a single, barbed stinger in the rear of their abdomens. The venom in the stinger usually produces pain and swelling but is rarely fatal unless a person is allergic to bee venom.

Zoom Fact: A bee can only sting once. When the bee tries to pull its stinger out of a victim, a part of the bee's body remains behind and the bee dies.

27 How are wasps different from bees?

Wasps and yellow jackets are insects that have longer and thinner bodies than bees. They build nests in the ground, in trees, and under the overhangs of buildings. Unlike bees, wasps do not have a barb on their stinger, so they can sting a person repeatedly. A large group of wasps attacking a person can cause a great deal of pain and even death.

Yellow Jacket

28 Which is the most dangerous insect in the United States?

Even though most people do not die from bee stings, the most dangerous insect is the honeybee. Honeybees cause about 50 deaths in the United States each year and kill more people than all the poisonous snakes combined. That's because so many more people in the United States are stung by honeybees than are ever bitten by a poisonous snake.

29 What are killer bees?

Killer bees are a kind of honeybee that originally came from Africa. These bees sting much more readily than ordinary honeybees. A single killer bee gives off a scent when it stings that attracts hundreds of other killer bees to the attack. The huge amount of bee venom injected from many killer bees can be enough to kill a victim.

30 What are fire ants?

Fire ants are stinging insects that can be found in many areas of the southern United States. The ants will instantly attack anyone who disturbs their large nests. They grasp a person's skin with their jaws and then insert a stinger, injecting venom from their poison sac. The ant then swivels around and stings seven or eight more times in a circle. The venom causes a fiery, burning pain.

31 Which is the most dangerous ant?

Bulldog ants of Australia are the most dangerous ants in the world. Their name comes from the way they grip something with their strong jaws, hang on, and sting repeatedly. These one inch long ants have a very painful stinger located in their abdomen.

32 Are there any poisonous butterflies or moths?

Some butterflies, such as Monarchs, are poisonous. The Monarch, and many moths, get their poison from the poisonous milkweed they eat when they are caterpillars. The small brown flannel moth caterpillar's body is covered by poisonous stinging hairs. If you touch that caterpillar, you will get a rash and blisters that last for days.

33 Are there any venomous beetles?

Blister beetles contain a chemical which is poisonous to people and animals. This chemical causes blistering on the skin. At one time blister beetles were killed, crushed, and used as a "cure" for sicknesses such as rheumatism.

(34) What is a Gila monster?

A Gila monster is a poisonous reptile that lives in the deserts of Mexico and the southwestern United States. Gila monsters can grow up to two feet long and have heavy bodies, large heads, and strong claws. Their bodies are covered by scales that look like shiny black or colored beads. The lizard doesn't inject the poison, but allows it to trickle into a bite that it holds for many minutes. A Gila monster bite can be fatal, but they rarely attack people.

35 Are any other lizards venomous?

Of the 3,000 different kinds of lizards, only two are poisonous: the Gila monster and the Mexican beaded lizard. The Mexican beaded lizard is larger and less colorful than the Gila monster, but it has a similar bite.

Red-spotted Newt

36 Are salamanders or newts venomous?

Most salamanders and newts have special glands on their heads, legs, or tails that produce poisons that coat their skin. For example, the red-spotted newt has poison glands in its neck. Its bold colors alert enemies that the newt is not a good meal for them to eat.

37 Are frogs and toads venomous?

Many frogs and toads are poisonous and sicken any animal that tries to eat them. Toads have poison sacs on their skin that look like warts. The toads taste terrible and the poison may even kill. The four-pound marine or cane toad of Australia can shoot poison in a fine spray from glands near its eyes.

38 Which animal is used to make poisonous darts?

More than 100 different kinds of poisonous dart frogs live in the forests of Central and South America. These tiny, brightly colored frogs are often less than half-an-inch long. Yet they produce a poison deadly enough to kill even large animals. For example, the yellow poison dart frog has enough poison in its body to kill dozens of people.

UNDER ᵀᴴᴱ SEA

㉟ Which is the most poisonous fish?

The most poisonous fish in the world is the stonefish of Australia and the southwest Pacific Ocean. The stonefish looks like a rock covered with patches of moss. It lies on the ocean floor waiting to eat small fish that come too close. If a person accidentally steps on a stonefish, the venomous spines on its top fin cause intense pain. The victim can die within hours unless treated immediately.

㊵ What is a scorpion fish?

There are about 300 different kinds of scorpion fish. They're also called lionfish, turkey fish, or zebra fish. They are usually brightly colored, small, slow-swimming fish

that have dozens of poisonous spines. The spines are not used to capture prey; they are defensive weapons against enemies. A scorpion fish sting causes intense pain but is rarely fatal to people.

④① Why is a puffer fish so deadly?

Puffer fish contain one of the deadliest poisons found in any animal. It's 25 times more powerful than that of the poison dart frog. But a puffer cannot inject the poison into another animal. The poison only kills people who eat a puffer. Puffers are safe to eat if prepared properly. But more than a dozen people die of puffer poisoning each year because the fish have not been properly cleaned.

④② Is a stingray venomous?

Stingrays are large, flat fish that swim through water like birds flying through air. Their stingers are sharp, barbed spines that grow from their tails. The stingers are coated with venom that causes a painful wound that heals slowly. Stingrays don't attack people, but people sometimes accidentally step on stingrays because they often lie on the ocean bottom or are buried in the sand.

43 What are sea wasps?

The box jellyfish, also called a sea wasp, is one of the most poisonous animals in the world. Sea wasps grow as large as basketballs with bundles of 10 to 60 six foot long stingers that float downward in the water. Each tentacle is armed with up to 5,000 stinging cells. Around the waters of northern Australia, there are as many as 70 reported deaths a year from sea wasp stings.

44 What is the Portuguese man-of-war?

The Portuguese man-of-war is usually thought to be a jellyfish but is actually a colony of several different kinds of animals. One kind forms a purple or blue air bladder about as large as a grapefruit that floats on water. Beneath this bladder dangle long, stinging tentacles which can hang down as far as 100 feet or more. The tentacles contain thousands of stinging cells that stun and kill small fish and other sea animals. The stingers are dangerous to people, too. The man-of-war is found in the Caribbean Sea.

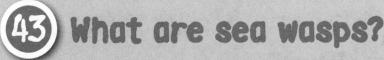

45 Why are sea urchins dangerous?

Sea urchins are spiny sea creatures that live in oceans all over the world. Their spines are long and sharp and protect the urchin against enemies. If a person steps on an urchin, the spines can cause a painful wound. Some kinds of sea urchins have venomous spines, but the wound is not usually deadly.

46 Can a starfish be venomous?

Most starfish are not venomous. The only venomous starfish is called the crown-of-thorns starfish, because it looks like a thorn bush. This starfish grows to over a foot across and has 10-20 arms. The skin of the crown-of-thorns starfish contains venomous glands that release poison on contact.

(47) Can an octopus be venomous?

The small blue-ringed octopus lives in Australian waters and has a very poisonous bite. The venom can cause death in just a few hours. But this octopus usually stays away from people and will only bite if attacked.

48 Are seashells venomous?

Because the shell is the outer covering of the animal, it is hard to think of a seashell as dangerous. Cone shells that live in the Indian and Pacific Oceans have hollow teeth at the end of a long, fleshy part that extends from the

bottom of their beautiful shells. The teeth inject fast-acting venom that is even deadly to people.

49 Is any mammal venomous?

Mammals are the least poisonous group of animals. The only larger mammal that is poisonous is the platypus of Australia. It has venomous hollow spurs on the inside of its rear feet which can cause severe pain and swelling that may last for months.

50 Are venomous animals good for anything?

Surprisingly, venom is used in medicine in a number of ways. It produces antivenom that blocks the effect of venom on humans. Venom is also used to treat strokes, stop clotting or break up blood clots in heart attack victims, and as a painkiller. In the future, we might discover even more ways that dangerous venoms can be used to help people.

INDEX